Introduction: A Journey of Transformation

I was today years old when I realized I had the power to change my life. This realization didn't come while I was on a successful sales call or standing on a stage receiving accolades. It happened in a much darker place—behind the bars of a prison cell.

As an Army veteran, I was trained to face adversity head-on, to push through challenges with grit and determination. But when I left the military, the structure and camaraderie I had relied on disappeared. Suddenly, I was adrift in a civilian world that felt alien and unwelcoming. I fell in with the wrong crowd, seeking comfort in the familiarity of a tight-knit group, even if they were heading down the wrong path. My decisions spiraled out of control, leading me to a six-year prison term.

Prison is a place where time stands still, where each day blends into the next in a monotonous blur. It's easy to let despair take hold, to believe that your life is over and that you'll never amount to anything again. And for a while, I did. I allowed my circumstances to define me, my mindset clouded by regret and anger.

But then, something changed. I was today years old when I realized that my thoughts and the people I surrounded myself with were the key to my transformation. It was a simple but profound shift in my perspective. I started to see my prison sentence not as a dead end, but as an opportunity for growth.

I began to read voraciously, devouring books on personal development, sales, and mindset. I sought out positive influences within the prison, other inmates who were committed to turning their lives around. We formed a support group, holding each other accountable and sharing our dreams for the future.

Slowly but surely, my mindset began to shift. I stopped seeing myself as a victim of my circumstances and started seeing myself as the architect of my future. I realized that the same principles that had guided me in the military—discipline, perseverance, and strategic thinking—could be applied to my personal and professional life.

When I was released, I was a different person. My past no longer defined me; my future did. I was ready to take on the world, armed with a new mindset and a determination to succeed.

This book is the culmination of my journey, a guide to help you achieve the same transformation I did. It's about realizing that you are never too old, too stuck, or too broken to change your life. You just need to change the way you think and the people you surround yourself with.

I was today years old when I discovered this truth, and you can be too. Let's embark on this journey together, transforming your mindset, your career, and your life.

Purpose of this book

1. Empowering Personal Transformation: This book aims to inspire and empower readers to realize that it's never too late to change their lives. Drawing from my own journey of transformation from a troubled post-military life and a prison sentence to a successful and fulfilling career, the book provides practical strategies and motivational insights. It encourages readers to shift their mindset, overcome limiting beliefs, and take proactive steps towards personal and professional growth. By sharing my story and the lessons learned along the way, I hope to show that anyone can reinvent themselves and achieve their goals, regardless of their past.

2. Building Resilient and Effective Sales Professionals: In addition to personal transformation, this book is a comprehensive guide for aspiring and current sales professionals looking to master their craft. It combines proven sales techniques with motivational strategies to help readers build resilience, improve their communication skills, and excel in their careers. Whether you're struggling with self-doubt, facing rejection, or seeking to enhance your sales performance, this book offers practical advice and actionable steps to help you succeed. By fostering a growth mindset and surrounding yourself with positive influences, you can transform not only your career but also your entire approach to life.

Chapter 1: Realizing your potential.

Discovering the Power Within

When I first left the military, I felt invincible. I had served my country, faced dangers head-on, and emerged physically unscathed. But the battles I fought within myself were far more daunting. Transitioning to civilian life was not the smooth ride I had envisioned. I lost the structured environment and camaraderie that had been my foundation, and I quickly found myself spiraling into a world of poor decisions and negative influences. This chapter is about that pivotal moment when I realized that the key to changing my life lay within me, and how you can uncover the same potential within yourself.

The Descent into Darkness

After my military service, the structure that had defined my daily life was gone. I was left to navigate a world that seemed to have no place for me. I fell in with the wrong crowd, seeking a sense of belonging and camaraderie that mirrored what I had in the Army. But this group was heading down a dark path, and I followed. Bad decisions snowballed, leading me to a six-year prison term—a consequence that could have easily shattered my spirit completely.

Inside those prison walls, I hit rock bottom. It was a place where hope was scarce and despair was abundant. Days turned into weeks, weeks into months, and the realization set in that I had to face the consequences of my actions. It was here, in this bleak environment, that the seeds of transformation were planted.

The Spark of Realization

One day, amidst the monotony and despair, I experienced a moment of clarity. It was a simple realization: I was today years old when I understood that my life didn't have to be defined by my past. I had the power to change my future. This revelation wasn't about a sudden grand epiphany, but rather a gradual understanding that the thoughts I harbored and the people I associated with were the architects of my destiny. I began to read anything I could get my hands on—books about personal development, sales, psychology, and success stories of people who had overcome insurmountable odds. These stories became my lifeline, a window into a world where change was possible. I learned that the mind is a powerful tool, capable of both great creation and destruction.

Steps to Realizing Your Potential

1. **Self-Awareness:** The first step in realizing your potential is developing self-awareness. Take an honest inventory of your strengths, weaknesses, and the patterns in your life that have led you to where you are today. Ask yourself tough questions: What are your core values? What drives you? What fears hold you back?

2. **Setting Intentions:** Once you have a clear understanding of yourself, set specific, intentional goals. These should be aligned with your core values and aspirations. Break them down into manageable steps and commit to taking action every day, no matter how small.

3. Changing Your Environment: Your environment plays a crucial role in shaping your mindset and behavior. Surround yourself with positive influences—people who inspire you, challenge you, and support your growth. In prison, I sought out individuals who, like me, were committed to turning their lives around. Together, we formed a support network that became our incubator for change. Holding eachother accountable.

4. Embracing a Growth Mindset: Understand that your abilities and intelligence can be developed through dedication and hard work. Embrace challenges, persist through setbacks, and see effort as a path to mastery. This growth mindset will open up new possibilities and help you to continuously evolve.

5. Taking Action: Knowledge without action is meaningless. Apply what you learn and take consistent steps towards your goals. In prison, my actions were small but significant: reading daily, engaging in positive conversations, and planning for a future I wanted to create. If I can do this inside the place where I started my journey what's your excuse? The fact is that the world is ran by people who aren't any smarter than your or me. They just think differently. You can train your brain.

Your Journey Begins Today

The moment you realize your potential is the moment you take control of your life. It's the day you stop letting your past dictate your future and start shaping your destiny with intention and purpose. You don't need to be in a prison cell to experience this transformation. It can happen anywhere, at any time—you just need to be open to it.

Remember, I was today years old when I discovered this truth, and you can be too. This book is your guide to uncovering the power within you, transforming your mindset, and achieving the success you deserve. The journey won't be easy, but it's undoubtedly worth it. Let today be the first step towards realizing your potential and creating the life you've always dreamed of.

Chapter 2: Overcoming Limiting Beliefs

Breaking Free from Mental Barriers

In the depths of my darkest days, it wasn't just the physical confinement of prison that held me back. The real chains were the limiting beliefs I harbored about myself—beliefs that I wasn't good enough, that I was destined to fail, that my past mistakes defined my future. This chapter is about identifying those limiting beliefs, understanding their origins, and, most importantly, breaking free from them.

Understanding Limiting Beliefs

Limiting beliefs are deeply ingrained assumptions and perceptions that hold you back from reaching your full potential. They are the mental barriers that tell you, "You can't do this," "You're not smart enough," or "People like you never succeed." These beliefs are often formed in childhood or during traumatic experiences, reinforced over time by negative experiences and the influence of others.

In my case, after leaving the military, I struggled with feelings of inadequacy. Despite my training and accomplishments, I doubted my ability to succeed in civilian life. My poor choices and subsequent imprisonment only solidified these negative beliefs. It wasn't until I began to challenge these thoughts that I realized they were not truths but rather self-imposed limitations.

Identifying Your Limiting Beliefs

1. Self-Reflection: The first step in overcoming limiting beliefs is to identify them. Start by reflecting on your life and pinpointing areas where you feel stuck or unfulfilled. Ask yourself:
   - What goals have I set aside because I believed I couldn't achieve them?
   - What opportunities have I missed due to fear or self-doubt?
   - What negative self-talk do I engage in regularly?

2. Writing It Down: Write down these beliefs as they come to mind. Seeing them on paper can help you analyze and confront them more objectively. For instance, you might write, "I believe I'm not smart enough to start my own business," or "I think I'll always be alone because I'm not worthy of love."

3. Tracing the Origins: Consider where these beliefs originated. Did they stem from a particular event, a series of failures, or the influence of someone in your life? Understanding the source can help you see that these beliefs are not innate truths but rather learned behaviors.

Challenging and Replacing Limiting Beliefs

1. Questioning the Beliefs: Challenge each limiting belief by asking:
- Is this belief based on facts or assumptions?
- What evidence do I have that contradicts this belief?
- How would my life change if I no longer held this belief?

In prison, I asked myself why I believed I couldn't succeed after my release. I realized that this belief was based on fear and past mistakes, not on my actual potential.

2. Reframing with Positive Affirmations: Replace limiting beliefs with positive affirmations. Instead of saying, "I can't," say, "I can." For example:
- "I'm not smart enough" becomes "I am capable and willing to learn."
- "I'll always be alone" becomes "I am deserving of love and companionship."

Affirmations should be specific, positive, and stated in the present tense. Repeat them daily to reinforce new, empowering beliefs.

3. Taking Action: Beliefs change through action. Start small and gradually take steps that contradict your limiting beliefs. If you believe you're not good at public speaking, join a local Toastmasters club and practice. Each small success will build your confidence and weaken the old, limiting belief.

Surrounding Yourself with Positivity

Your environment plays a crucial role in shaping your beliefs. Surround yourself with positive influences—people who support and encourage your growth. In prison, I sought out other inmates who were focused on self-improvement. We shared books, discussed our goals, and held each other accountable.

In your life, seek mentors, join supportive communities, and engage with content that uplifts and inspires you. The more you immerse yourself in positivity, the easier it will be to maintain a mindset of growth and possibility.

Embracing the New You

Overcoming limiting beliefs is not a one-time event but an ongoing process. As you grow and encounter new challenges, old doubts may resurface. When they do, remind yourself of your past victories and the strength you possess. Reaffirm your positive beliefs and continue to take action.

Remember, I was today years old when I realized I could change my life by changing my beliefs. You have that same power within you. By identifying, challenging, and replacing your limiting beliefs, you can break free from mental barriers and unlock your true potential. Let today be the day you start believing in the limitless possibilities that lie ahead.

As we continue this journey together, you'll gain more tools and insights to build on this foundation. Your potential is vast, and your future is bright. Embrace it with an open mind and a fearless heart.

Chapter 3: Embracing a Growth Mindset

The Power of Perspective

Throughout my life, I faced numerous challenges and setbacks. From the rigors of military service to the confinement of a prison cell, each experience tested my resilience and resolve. However, the most profound change came not from my external circumstances but from a shift in my internal perspective. This chapter is about embracing a growth mindset—a belief that your abilities and intelligence can be developed through dedication, hard work, and a willingness to learn from experiences.

Fixed Mindset vs. Growth Mindset

Psychologist Carol Dweck's research on mindsets provides a powerful framework for understanding how our beliefs about ourselves can influence our success. According to Dweck, people generally operate with one of two mindsets: fixed or growth.

1. Fixed Mindset:

Individuals with a fixed mindset believe that their talents, intelligence, and abilities are static traits. They often think:

"I am who I am, and I can't change that."
"I'm either good at something or I'm not."
"Failure is a reflection of my inherent limitations."

2. Growth Mindset:

Those with a growth mindset believe that their abilities can be developed through effort, learning, and persistence. They think:

"I can improve with practice and effort."
"Challenges help me grow."
"Failure is a learning opportunity."

Adopting a growth mindset was crucial in my transformation. It allowed me to see each setback as a stepping stone rather than a stumbling block.

Developing a Growth Mindset

1. Embrace Challenges:

Challenges are opportunities for growth. Instead of avoiding difficult tasks, tackle them head-on. View each challenge as a chance to learn and improve. When I was in prison, I faced the challenge of rebuilding my life from scratch. Embracing this challenge, rather than succumbing to despair, set me on the path to self-improvement.

2. Learn from Criticism:

Constructive criticism is valuable feedback that can help you grow. Instead of taking criticism personally, analyze it objectively. What can you learn from it? How can it help you improve? During my journey, I learned to listen to feedback from mentors and peers, using it to refine my skills and strategies.

3. Persist in the Face of Setbacks:

Persistence is key to developing a growth mindset. Understand that setbacks and failures are part of the learning process. When faced with obstacles, remind yourself of your long-term goals and keep pushing forward. In prison, every day presented new challenges, but persistence kept me focused on my ultimate goal of transformation.

4. Cultivate Curiosity:

A curious mind is always learning. Cultivate a habit of asking questions, seeking new knowledge, and exploring different perspectives. Curiosity drives innovation and creativity, helping you to find unique solutions to problems. My curiosity led me to read extensively, gaining insights that fueled my personal growth.

5. Celebrate Effort Over Results:

Focus on the effort you put in rather than the immediate results. Recognize and celebrate your hard work and dedication, regardless of the outcome. This reinforces the belief that effort leads to improvement and success. During my transformation, I celebrated small victories, like completing a book or learning a new skill, which motivated me to keep going.

Practical Exercises for Cultivating a Growth Mindset

1. Reflection Journaling:
Keep a journal to reflect on your daily experiences. Write about challenges you faced, how you handled them, and what you learned. This practice helps reinforce the growth mindset by highlighting your progress and learning.

2. Goal Setting and Planning:
Set specific, achievable goals that align with your growth objectives. Break these goals down into smaller, manageable tasks and create a plan to achieve them. Regularly review and adjust your goals as you progress.

3. Affirmations and Visualization:
Use positive affirmations to reinforce your growth mindset. Visualize yourself overcoming challenges and achieving your goals. This mental practice prepares your mind for success and boosts your confidence.

4. Seek Feedback:
Actively seek feedback from others, whether it's from mentors, peers, or friends. Use this feedback to identify areas for improvement and to guide your development.

5. Embrace Lifelong Learning:
Commit to lifelong learning by continuously seeking new knowledge and skills. Attend workshops, take courses, read books, and engage in activities that expand your horizons.

Your Growth Journey Begins Now
Embracing a growth mindset is a powerful step towards achieving your full potential. It transforms how you perceive challenges, setbacks, and success. By adopting this mindset, you open yourself up to endless possibilities for growth and improvement.

Remember, the journey of personal and professional growth is ongoing. It requires dedication, persistence, and a willingness to learn from every experience. I was today years old when I embraced the power of a growth mindset, and it changed my life profoundly. You can make this shift too, and when you do, you'll unlock a world of opportunities and potential.

As you continue reading, you'll find more tools and strategies to support your journey. Keep an open mind, stay curious, and embrace every challenge as a chance to grow. Your potential is limitless, and your future is bright. Let's continue this journey together, transforming your mindset and achieving the success you deserve.

Chapter 4: Understanding the Sales Process

The Art and Science of Selling

Sales is often viewed as a mysterious art reserved for those with the "gift of gab." However, successful selling is a blend of art and science—a structured process that, when mastered, can lead to extraordinary results. In this chapter, we will break down the sales process into its key stages, providing you with actionable advice and strategies to excel at each step. Whether you're new to sales or looking to refine your skills, understanding and mastering this process is crucial to your success.

The Key Stages of the Sales Process

1. Prospecting:

Prospecting is the foundation of the sales process. It involves identifying and reaching out to potential customers who may benefit from your product or service. Effective prospecting ensures that you spend your time and energy on the most promising leads.

Strategies for Effective Prospecting:

Define Your Ideal Customer: Create a detailed profile of your ideal customer, including demographics, behaviors, and pain points. This helps you target your efforts more effectively.

Utilize Multiple Channels: Leverage a variety of channels such as social media, networking events, referrals, and cold calling to reach potential customers.

Consistent Follow-Up: Keep track of your prospects and follow up regularly. Persistence often pays off in sales.

2. Qualifying:

Qualifying is the process of determining whether a prospect is a good fit for your product or service. This step saves you time by ensuring you focus on leads that are most likely to convert into sales.

Criteria for Qualifying Prospects:

Need: Does the prospect have a need or problem that your product can solve?

Budget: Can the prospect afford your product or service?

Authority: Does the prospect have the authority to make a purchasing decision?

Timeline: What is the prospect's timeframe for making a decision?

3. Presenting:

Presenting involves showcasing your product or service to the qualified prospect in a way that addresses their specific needs and demonstrates value. This is where your preparation and understanding of the prospect come into play.

Effective Presentation Techniques:

Tailor Your Message: Customize your presentation to address the prospect's unique needs and pain points.
Focus on Benefits: Highlight the benefits and value of your product, not just the features. Explain how it will solve their problems or improve their situation.
Engage the Prospect: Ask questions, encourage interaction, and listen actively to the prospect's responses.

4. Handling Objections:

Objections are a natural part of the sales process. Prospects may raise concerns about price, product fit, or other factors. Handling objections effectively can turn potential deal-breakers into opportunities for further discussion.

Strategies for Handling Objections:

Listen Actively: Let the prospect fully express their concerns without interrupting.
Empathize: Show understanding and empathy towards their concerns.
Address Specifically: Provide clear, concise responses that address the specific objection.
Reinforce Value: Remind the prospect of the value and benefits of your product.

5. Closing:

Closing is the stage where you guide the prospect to make a purchasing decision. This step requires confidence, skill, and an understanding of the prospect's buying signals.

Effective Closing Techniques:

Assumptive Close: Act as if the prospect has already decided to buy and move forward with the next steps.
Urgency Close: Create a sense of urgency by highlighting limited availability or time-sensitive offers.
Alternative Close: Present two options, both leading to a sale, and ask the prospect to choose.

6. Follow-Up:

The sales process doesn't end with closing the deal. Following up with customers ensures long-term satisfaction, encourages repeat business, and generates referrals.

Follow-Up Best Practices:

Express Gratitude: Thank the customer for their purchase and express your appreciation.
Provide Support: Ensure the customer knows how to use the product and has access to support if needed.
Stay in Touch: Regularly check in with the customer to maintain the relationship and identify future needs.

Putting It All Together

Understanding and mastering each stage of the sales process is essential for success. Let's revisit a real-life scenario to illustrate how these stages come together. When I was starting over after my release, I faced the daunting task of rebuilding my life and career. I realized that selling wasn't just about pushing a product—it was about understanding people, building relationships, and providing value.

Through trial and error, I refined my approach. I started by identifying potential clients who could benefit from my services, understanding their needs, and presenting tailored solutions. When objections arose, I listened, empathized, and addressed their concerns with confidence. Closing deals became a natural outcome of building trust and demonstrating value. Follow-up was critical to maintaining these relationships and building a network of satisfied customers who were more than willing to refer me to others.

Actionable Steps to Master the Sales Process

Create a Prospect List: Develop a list of potential clients based on your ideal customer profile.

Qualify Your Leads: Use the qualifying criteria to focus on the most promising prospects.

Prepare Your Presentation: Tailor your message to address the specific needs and pain points of your prospects.

Practice Handling Objections: Role-play common objections with a colleague or mentor to build confidence.

Develop Closing Strategies: Identify which closing techniques work best for you and practice them regularly.

Implement a Follow-Up System: Create a system for regular follow-ups to ensure customer satisfaction and encourage repeat business.

Mastering the sales process is an ongoing journey of learning and adaptation. Each stage requires dedication, practice, and a willingness to learn from every experience. Remember, sales is not just about transactions—it's about building lasting relationships based on trust and value. As you refine your skills and strategies, you'll find that success in sales is not just achievable, but repeatable.

By understanding and mastering the sales process, you are well on your way to transforming your career and achieving the success you deserve. Keep pushing forward, stay curious, and never stop learning. Your potential is limitless, and your journey is just beginning.

Chapter 5: Building Meaningful Relationships
The Heart of Sales and Success

In both life and sales, relationships are the cornerstone of success. Genuine, meaningful relationships create trust, foster loyalty, and open doors to opportunities that would otherwise remain closed. This chapter delves into the art of building and nurturing relationships, providing you with practical strategies to connect deeply with others, whether they are clients, colleagues, or mentors.

The Importance of Authenticity

Authenticity is the foundation of any strong relationship. People can sense when you are genuine and when you are not. Authenticity builds trust and credibility, both of which are crucial in sales and personal interactions.

1. Be Yourself:

Embrace your true self in all interactions. Authenticity means being honest about your strengths and weaknesses, and not pretending to be someone you are not. This openness encourages others to be authentic as well, creating a deeper connection.

2. Show Genuine Interest:

Show a genuine interest in others' lives, needs, and aspirations. Ask questions, listen actively, and remember details about what they share with you. This demonstrates that you value them as individuals, not just as potential sales or connections.

3. Consistent Integrity:

Always act with integrity. Keep your promises, be honest in your dealings, and maintain high ethical standards. Integrity builds long-term trust, which is essential for lasting relationships.

Effective Communication Skills

Effective communication is key to building and maintaining relationships. It involves not just speaking, but also listening, understanding, and responding appropriately.

1. Active Listening:

Listen more than you speak. Active listening involves fully concentrating on what the other person is saying, understanding their message, and responding thoughtfully. This makes the other person feel valued and heard.

2. Empathy:

Practice empathy by putting yourself in the other person's shoes. Understand their feelings, perspectives, and concerns. Empathy builds deeper connections and fosters mutual respect.

3. Clear and Honest Communication:

Be clear and honest in your communication. Avoid jargon and ambiguity. If you don't know the answer to a question, admit it and find out. Honesty fosters trust and respect.

Networking with Purpose

Networking is not about collecting business cards or adding connections on social media. It's about creating meaningful, mutually beneficial relationships.

1. Quality Over Quantity:

Focus on building a few strong, meaningful relationships rather than trying to connect with everyone. Quality relationships are more likely to lead to opportunities and support.

2. Provide Value:

In every interaction, look for ways to provide value to the other person. This could be through sharing information, offering assistance, or making introductions to helpful contacts. When you provide value, people are more likely to reciprocate.

3. Follow-Up:

Follow-up is crucial in networking. After meeting someone new, send a personalized message or email to thank them for their time and express your interest in staying connected. Regular follow-ups help maintain and strengthen relationships over time.

Building Client Relationships

In sales, building strong client relationships is essential for repeat business and referrals. Clients who trust and value you are more likely to continue doing business with you and recommend you to others.

1. Understand Their Needs:
Take the time to understand your clients' needs, goals, and challenges. This allows you to tailor your solutions to their specific situations, demonstrating that you genuinely care about their success.

2. Stay in Touch:
Maintain regular contact with your clients, even when you are not trying to make a sale. Share relevant information, check in on their progress, and offer assistance when needed. This keeps you top-of-mind and reinforces the relationship.

3. Go the Extra Mile:
Always look for ways to exceed your clients' expectations. Whether it's delivering exceptional service, offering additional support, or providing unexpected value, going the extra mile builds loyalty and strengthens the relationship.

Mentorship and Learning

Mentorship plays a significant role in personal and professional growth. Building relationships with mentors can provide you with valuable guidance, support, and insight.

1. Seek Out Mentors:
Identify individuals who have the experience and qualities you admire. Reach out to them with genuine respect and interest in learning from their experiences. Be clear about what you hope to gain from the mentorship.

2. Be a Good Mentee:
Show your appreciation for your mentor's time and insights. Be punctual, prepared, and open to feedback. Take action on their advice and share your progress with them.

3. Give Back:
As you grow and gain experience, look for opportunities to mentor others. Sharing your knowledge and experiences not only helps others but also reinforces your own learning and growth.

The Role of Technology in Relationship Building

Technology can be a powerful tool for building and maintaining relationships, especially in today's digital age.

1. Use Social Media Wisely:
Leverage social media platforms to connect with others, share valuable content, and engage in meaningful conversations. Be authentic and professional in your online interactions.

2. Customer Relationship Management (CRM) Tools:
Utilize CRM tools to keep track of your interactions with clients and prospects. These tools help you manage follow-ups, remember important details, and provide personalized service.

3. Virtual Meetings:
In the age of remote work, virtual meetings have become essential. Use video conferencing tools to maintain face-to-face interactions, build rapport, and stay connected with clients and colleagues.

Your Relationship-Building Journey

Building meaningful relationships takes time, effort, and dedication. It requires a commitment to authenticity, effective communication, and providing value. Whether you are connecting with clients, colleagues, or mentors, the relationships you build will be the foundation of your success.

Remember, I was today years old when I realized the power of meaningful relationships. You can start building these relationships today. As you continue this journey, focus on being genuine, listening actively, and always looking for ways to provide value. These principles will not only help you succeed in sales but will also enrich your personal and professional life.

Let's continue this journey together, transforming not only our careers but also our lives through the power of meaningful relationships. Your potential is limitless, and your future is bright. Embrace it with an open heart and a willingness to connect deeply with others.

Chapter 6: Setting and Achieving Goals
The Roadmap to Success

Setting and achieving goals is a fundamental component of personal and professional success. Goals provide direction, motivation, and a clear measure of progress. This chapter will guide you through the process of setting meaningful goals and provide practical strategies to achieve them. By the end of this chapter, you'll be equipped with the tools to turn your aspirations into reality.

The Importance of Goal Setting

Goals give you something to strive for, a target to aim at. They help you focus your efforts and resources, making your actions more purposeful and directed. Without goals, it's easy to drift aimlessly, making little progress and feeling unfulfilled. Here's why goal setting is crucial:

1. Clarity and Focus:
Goals help you define what you want to achieve and provide a clear focus for your efforts.

2. Motivation and Drive:
Having specific goals keeps you motivated and driven, especially during challenging times.

3. Measurement of Progress:
Goals provide benchmarks for measuring your progress and accomplishments.

4. Accountability:
Setting goals helps you hold yourself accountable for your actions and decisions.

SMART Goals Framework

The SMART framework is a widely-used method for setting effective goals. SMART stands for Specific, Measurable, Achievable, Relevant, and Time-bound. Let's break down each component:

1. Specific:
Your goals should be clear and specific, answering the questions of what you want to accomplish and why it's important.

Example: Instead of saying "I want to improve my sales," specify "I want to increase my sales by 20% within the next six months by focusing on upselling and cross-selling to existing clients."

2. Measurable:
Your goals should include criteria for measuring progress. This helps you stay on track and recognize when you've achieved your goal.

Example: "I will track my sales numbers weekly and compare them to my targets to ensure I'm on pace."

3. Achievable:
Your goals should be realistic and attainable. Stretch yourself, but don't set goals that are impossible to achieve.

Example: "Given my current sales figures and resources, a 20% increase in six months is challenging but doable."

4. Relevant:
Your goals should align with your broader objectives and values. They should be important to you and contribute to your overall success.

Example: "Increasing my sales will help me achieve my career advancement goals and increase my earnings."

5. Time-bound:
Your goals should have a clear deadline to create a sense of urgency and prompt timely action.

Example: "I will achieve this 20% sales increase by December 31st."

Steps to Setting and Achieving Goals

1. Identify Your Priorities:
Start by identifying what's most important to you in your personal and professional life. What do you want to achieve in the short term and long term? Reflect on your values, passions, and aspirations.

2. Write Down Your Goals:
Writing down your goals makes them tangible and helps you commit to achieving them. Be specific and use the SMART framework.

3. Break Down Goals into Actionable Steps:
Large goals can be overwhelming. Break them down into smaller, manageable tasks. Create a step-by-step plan detailing what you need to do to achieve each goal.

4. Set Milestones and Deadlines:
Set intermediate milestones and deadlines to track your progress. This keeps you motivated and ensures that you're moving forward.

5. Monitor Your Progress:
Regularly review your progress toward your goals. Adjust your plans as needed based on what you learn. Celebrate small wins to keep yourself motivated.

6. Stay Flexible and Adapt:
Be prepared to adjust your goals and plans as circumstances change. Flexibility is key to overcoming obstacles and staying on track.

Overcoming Common Obstacles
Achieving goals often involves overcoming various obstacles. Here are some common challenges and strategies to address them:

1. Procrastination:
Break tasks into smaller steps and set short-term deadlines to create a sense of urgency. Use techniques like the Pomodoro Technique to stay focused and productive.

2. Lack of Motivation:
Remind yourself of the reasons why you set the goal. Visualize the benefits of achieving it and the consequences of not. Surround yourself with supportive and motivating people.

3. Fear of Failure:
Accept that failure is a part of the learning process. Use setbacks as opportunities to learn and improve. Focus on progress, not perfection.

4. Distractions:
Identify and eliminate distractions. Create a dedicated workspace, set boundaries, and use tools to stay organized and focused.

5. Lack of Resources:
Identify the resources you need to achieve your goals. This could include time, money, skills, or support from others. Develop a plan to acquire these resources.

Real-Life Application

To illustrate the process, let's revisit a personal example. After my release from prison, I faced the daunting task of rebuilding my life. Setting and achieving goals was crucial to my transformation.

1. Specific Goal:
I wanted to find stable employment within three months to regain financial independence and stability.

2. Measurable:
I aimed to apply to at least five jobs per week and network with at least three new contacts weekly.

3. Achievable:
Given my skills and experience, I set a realistic target to find a job within my qualifications and interests.

4. Relevant:
Securing employment was a critical step toward rebuilding my life and achieving long-term success.

5. Time-bound:
I set a deadline of three months to secure a job.

By following these steps and overcoming obstacles like rejection and self-doubt, I successfully found employment within my target timeframe. This experience reinforced the power of setting and achieving goals, motivating me to continue striving for success.

Your Path to Achievement

Setting and achieving goals is a dynamic process that requires commitment, flexibility, and perseverance. By using the SMART framework and following the steps outlined in this chapter, you can turn your aspirations into actionable plans and achieve the success you desire.

Remember, I was today years old when I realized the transformative power of goal setting. You too can start today, defining your goals and taking the first steps toward achieving them. As you continue on this journey, you'll find that each goal achieved builds momentum, leading to greater accomplishments and a fulfilling life.

Let's continue this journey together, setting and achieving goals that bring us closer to our dreams and aspirations. Your potential is limitless, and your future is bright. Embrace it with determination and a clear vision of what you want to achieve.

Chapter 7: Cultivating Resilience

The Importance of Resilience

Life is filled with challenges, setbacks, and unexpected events. The ability to bounce back from adversity and continue moving forward is known as resilience. Resilience is not just about enduring hardship; it's about emerging from difficult situations stronger and more determined. This chapter explores the nature of resilience and offers strategies to cultivate and strengthen this vital trait.

Understanding Resilience

Resilience is the capacity to recover quickly from difficulties and adapt to change. It involves maintaining a positive outlook, managing stress effectively, and continuing to pursue goals despite obstacles. Resilience is not an inherent trait; it can be developed and strengthened over time.

1. Adaptability:
Resilient people are flexible and can adapt to new circumstances and challenges. They view change as an opportunity for growth rather than a threat.

2. Emotional Regulation:
Resilience involves managing emotions effectively. This means staying calm under pressure, maintaining perspective, and not allowing negative emotions to take over.

3. Problem-Solving Skills:
Resilient individuals approach problems proactively. They break down challenges into manageable parts and develop practical solutions.

4. Support Systems:
Having a network of supportive relationships is crucial for resilience. Friends, family, mentors, and colleagues can provide emotional support, advice, and encouragement.

Building Resilience

Building resilience is a process that involves developing certain habits, mindsets, and behaviors. Here are key strategies to help you cultivate resilience:

1. Develop a Positive Mindset:

Focus on Strengths: Recognize and build on your strengths and successes. This boosts your confidence and helps you face new challenges.

Practice Gratitude: Regularly reflect on the positive aspects of your life and express gratitude. This shifts your focus from what's wrong to what's right.

Reframe Challenges: View challenges as opportunities to learn and grow. This positive reframing helps you approach difficulties with a constructive attitude.

2. Manage Stress Effectively:

Mindfulness and Relaxation: Practice mindfulness, meditation, or other relaxation techniques to manage stress and maintain mental clarity.

Healthy Lifestyle: Maintain a healthy lifestyle through regular exercise, balanced nutrition, and adequate sleep. Physical well-being is closely linked to emotional resilience.

Time Management: Organize your time and prioritize tasks to reduce stress and avoid feeling overwhelmed.

3. Strengthen Problem-Solving Skills:

Break Down Problems: When faced with a challenge, break it down into smaller, more manageable parts. Tackle each part step by step.

Seek Solutions: Focus on finding solutions rather than dwelling on problems. Brainstorm multiple approaches and choose the best one.

Learn from Experience: Reflect on past challenges and what you learned from them. Use these lessons to approach new problems more effectively.

4. Build Strong Relationships:

Nurture Connections: Invest time and effort in building and maintaining relationships with supportive people. These connections provide emotional support and practical assistance.

Seek Help: Don't hesitate to seek help when needed. Asking for support is a sign of strength, not weakness.

Offer Support: Be there for others. Providing support strengthens your relationships and creates a reciprocal network of help.

Real-Life Resilience

Reflecting on my own journey, resilience played a critical role in my transformation. After leaving the army and facing the challenges of civilian life, my poor mindset and associations led to a six-year prison term. It was during this time that I made the conscious decision to change my life.

In prison, I faced numerous adversities, but I chose to view my situation as an opportunity for growth. I focused on improving myself, reading extensively, and learning new skills. I managed stress through exercise and mindfulness, which helped me maintain a positive outlook. Most importantly, I built strong relationships with supportive individuals who encouraged and guided me.

These experiences taught me that resilience is not just about enduring hardships but about actively working to overcome them and emerge stronger. By developing a positive mindset, managing stress, improving problem-solving skills, and building a support network, I was able to transform my life and achieve my goals.

Practical Exercises to Build Resilience

1. Journaling:
Keep a journal to reflect on your experiences, challenges, and how you overcame them. This practice helps you gain perspective and recognize your resilience.

2. Mindfulness Meditation:
Practice mindfulness meditation to stay grounded and manage stress. Even a few minutes of meditation each day can significantly improve your emotional regulation.

3. Goal Setting:
Set small, achievable goals that help you build confidence and a sense of accomplishment. As you achieve these goals, set new ones to continue challenging yourself.

4. Build a Support Network:
Identify and nurture relationships with supportive people in your life. Schedule regular check-ins with friends, family, or mentors to maintain these connections.

5. Self-Care Routine:
Develop a self-care routine that includes activities you enjoy and that help you relax. This could include exercise, hobbies, or spending time in nature.

Your Journey to Resilience

Building resilience is an ongoing journey that requires commitment and effort. It's about developing the habits and mindsets that enable you to bounce back from setbacks and continue moving forward. Remember, resilience is not about never facing difficulties; it's about how you respond to them.

I was today years old when I realized the true power of resilience. By cultivating resilience, you can transform challenges into opportunities for growth and achieve your goals despite the obstacles.

As you continue reading and applying the strategies in this book, you'll find that resilience becomes a natural part of your life. Embrace this journey, and remember that every setback is an opportunity to become stronger and more determined. Your potential is limitless, and your future is bright. Let's continue this journey together, building resilience and achieving the success you deserve.

Chapter 8: The Power of Mindset

Introduction to Mindset

Your mindset, or your beliefs and attitudes about yourself and the world, plays a significant role in determining your success and happiness. In this chapter, we will explore the concept of mindset and how it influences your behavior, decisions, and outcomes. By understanding the power of mindset, you can unlock your full potential and achieve extraordinary results.

Fixed vs. Growth Mindset

Psychologist Carol Dweck introduced the concept of fixed and growth mindsets. Individuals with a fixed mindset believe that their abilities and intelligence are fixed traits, while those with a growth mindset believe that they can improve and develop through effort and perseverance.

1. Fixed Mindset:

Attributes Success to Innate Talent: People with a fixed mindset believe that success is primarily determined by innate abilities and talent.

Avoids Challenges: They tend to avoid challenges that may expose their limitations, fearing failure.

Views Effort as Fruitless: Individuals with a fixed mindset often see effort as pointless, believing that if they have to try hard, they must not be naturally talented.

Reacts Negatively to Criticism: Criticism is taken personally and seen as a reflection of their inherent abilities, leading to defensiveness or avoidance.

Gives Up Easily: When faced with setbacks or failures, those with a fixed mindset are more likely to give up, believing that they lack the necessary talent to succeed.

2. Growth Mindset:

Embraces Challenges: People with a growth mindset see challenges as opportunities for growth and learning. They welcome new experiences and are not afraid to step out of their comfort zone.

Values Effort and Persistence: Effort is seen as essential for mastery and improvement. Individuals with a growth mindset understand that skills can be developed through dedication and hard work.

Sees Criticism as Constructive Feedback: Criticism is viewed as valuable feedback that provides insights for improvement. Those with a growth mindset use criticism as an opportunity to learn and grow.

Persists in the Face of Setbacks: Setbacks and failures are seen as temporary setbacks, not permanent limitations. People with a growth mindset are resilient and persistent, bouncing back from setbacks with renewed determination.

Cultivating a Growth Mindset

The good news is that mindset is not fixed; it can be changed and cultivated over time. Here are strategies to develop a growth mindset:

1. Embrace Challenges:

Step Out of Your Comfort Zone: Challenge yourself by trying new things and taking on tasks that stretch your abilities.

View Challenges as Opportunities: Instead of fearing challenges, see them as opportunities for growth and learning.

2. Value Effort and Persistence:

Celebrate Effort: Focus on your effort and hard work rather than just the outcome. Recognize that progress is made through consistent effort over time.

Learn from Failure: Instead of seeing failure as a reflection of your abilities, view it as a stepping stone to success. Analyze what went wrong and what you can do differently next time.

3. Cultivate a Positive Inner Dialogue:

Challenge Negative Self-Talk: Pay attention to your inner dialogue and challenge negative self-limiting beliefs. Replace them with more empowering and growth-oriented thoughts.

Practice Self-Compassion: Treat yourself with kindness and understanding, especially in times of difficulty or failure. Acknowledge that setbacks are a natural part of the learning process.

4. Seek Growth-Oriented Feedback:

Welcome Feedback: Seek feedback from others, whether it's from mentors, colleagues, or peers. Use feedback as an opportunity to identify areas for improvement and growth.

Focus on Learning: Shift your focus from seeking validation to seeking opportunities for learning and development.

5. Surround Yourself with Growth-Minded Individuals:

Choose Your Circle Wisely: Surround yourself with people who have a growth mindset and who support your aspirations. Their positive influence and encouragement can help reinforce your own growth mindset.

Real-Life Examples of Mindset in Action

Throughout history, countless individuals have demonstrated the power of mindset in achieving extraordinary feats:

1. Thomas Edison:

Growth Mindset: Despite facing thousands of failures in his attempts to invent the light bulb, Edison maintained a growth mindset, viewing each failure as a step closer to success. He famously said, "I have not failed. I've just found 10,000 ways that won't work."

2. Oprah Winfrey:

Growth Mindset: Oprah overcame a difficult childhood and numerous setbacks to become one of the most influential media moguls in the world. She attributes her success to her growth mindset and resilience in the face of adversity.

3. Michael Jordan:

Growth Mindset: Widely regarded as one of the greatest basketball players of all time, Michael Jordan faced numerous setbacks and challenges throughout his career. However, his growth mindset and relentless work ethic enabled him to overcome obstacles and achieve unparalleled success.

Your Mindset Journey

Your mindset has the power to shape your reality and determine your level of success and fulfillment. By cultivating a growth mindset, you can unlock your full potential and achieve extraordinary results. Remember, your mindset is not fixed; it can be changed and developed over time with dedication and effort.

As you continue on your journey, embrace challenges, value effort and persistence, cultivate a positive inner dialogue, seek growth-oriented feedback, and surround yourself with like-minded individuals. By doing so, you'll not only achieve your goals but also lead a more fulfilling and meaningful life.

I was today years old when I realized the transformative power of mindset. Now, armed with the knowledge and strategies in this chapter, you have the tools to cultivate a growth mindset and unlock your full potential. Embrace this journey with optimism and determination, knowing that your mindset is the key to achieving the success and happiness you deserve.

Chapter 9: The Art of Self-Reflection

Introduction to Self-Reflection

Self-reflection is the process of looking inward to examine your thoughts, feelings, and behaviors. It involves taking a step back to assess yourself objectively and gain insight into your strengths, weaknesses, values, and goals. In this chapter, we will explore the importance of self-reflection and how it can lead to personal growth, self-awareness, and improved decision-making.

The Benefits of Self-Reflection

Self-reflection offers numerous benefits that contribute to personal and professional development:

1. Increased Self-Awareness:

Self-reflection allows you to gain a deeper understanding of yourself, including your motivations, values, and beliefs. This self-awareness is the foundation for personal growth and meaningful change.

2. Improved Decision-Making:

By examining past experiences and outcomes, you can identify patterns and lessons learned that inform future decisions. Self-reflection helps you make more informed and intentional choices aligned with your values and goals.

3. Enhanced Problem-Solving Skills:

Self-reflection encourages critical thinking and analysis, enabling you to approach problems more effectively. By examining different perspectives and considering alternative solutions, you can find creative solutions to challenges.

4. Greater Emotional Intelligence:

Self-reflection fosters emotional intelligence by helping you recognize and regulate your emotions. By understanding your emotional triggers and responses, you can manage stress, build resilience, and improve interpersonal relationships.

5. Personal Growth and Development:

Self-reflection is a catalyst for personal growth and development. By identifying areas for improvement and setting goals for self-improvement, you can strive to become the best version of yourself.

Techniques for Self-Reflection

There are various techniques you can use to engage in self-reflection:

1. Journaling:
Writing in a journal allows you to record your thoughts, feelings, and experiences. Regular journaling provides a space for self-expression and introspection, helping you gain clarity and insight into your life.

2. Meditation and Mindfulness:
Practicing meditation and mindfulness allows you to quiet the mind and focus inward. By observing your thoughts and feelings without judgment, you can cultivate self-awareness and develop a deeper understanding of yourself.

3. Self-Questioning:
Asking yourself probing questions prompts deeper reflection. Questions such as "What am I grateful for?" "What did I learn today?" and "What could I have done differently?" encourage introspection and self-discovery.

4. Feedback Seeking:
Seeking feedback from others provides an external perspective that can complement self-reflection. Ask trusted friends, colleagues, or mentors for constructive feedback on your strengths, weaknesses, and areas for growth.

5. Regular Check-Ins:
Schedule regular check-ins with yourself to assess your progress and well-being. Set aside dedicated time for reflection, whether it's daily, weekly, or monthly, to ensure you stay connected with yourself.

Incorporating Self-Reflection into Your Routine

To make self-reflection a regular practice, consider the following strategies:

1. Schedule Dedicated Time:
Set aside dedicated time in your schedule for self-reflection. Treat it as a non-negotiable appointment with yourself, just like you would any other important commitment.

2. Create a Reflective Environment:
Find a quiet and comfortable space where you can engage in self-reflection without distractions. Create a calming atmosphere with soft lighting, comfortable seating, and any other elements that help you relax and focus.

3. Set Clear Intentions:
Before engaging in self-reflection, set clear intentions for what you hope to achieve. Whether it's gaining clarity on a specific issue, identifying areas for improvement, or simply checking in with yourself, having a clear focus enhances the effectiveness of your reflection.

4. Practice Non-Judgment:
Approach self-reflection with an open and non-judgmental attitude. Avoid harsh self-criticism and instead cultivate self-compassion and acceptance. Remember that self-reflection is about growth, not perfection.

5. Review and Adjust:
Regularly review your reflections and use them to inform your actions and decisions. Identify patterns, lessons learned, and areas for adjustment or improvement. Continuously iterate and refine your self-reflection process based on your experiences.

Real-Life Application of Self-Reflection

Reflecting on my own journey, self-reflection played a crucial role in my personal and professional development. During challenging times, such as my transition from the army to civilian life and my subsequent incarceration, self-reflection provided me with clarity, insight, and direction. By examining my thoughts, feelings, and behaviors, I was able to identify areas for growth, set goals, and take proactive steps toward positive change.

Your Self-Reflection Journey

Self-reflection is a powerful tool for personal growth, self-awareness, and decision-making. By incorporating self-reflection into your routine and practicing various techniques, you can deepen your understanding of yourself, enhance your problem-solving skills, and cultivate resilience.

As you embark on your self-reflection journey, remember that it's a process of continuous learning and growth. Be patient and compassionate with yourself, and allow space for exploration and discovery. Embrace the opportunity to learn from your experiences, celebrate your successes, and navigate challenges with wisdom and insight.

I was today years old when I realized the transformative power of self-reflection. Now, armed with the knowledge and strategies in this chapter, you have the tools to embark on your own self-reflection journey. Embrace it with an open heart and a curious mind, knowing that each moment of introspection brings you closer to a deeper understanding of yourself and a more fulfilling life.

Chapter 10: Building Resilience Through Adversity

Introduction to Resilience

Resilience is the capacity to recover quickly from difficulties and adapt in the face of adversity, trauma, or significant stress. It involves maintaining flexibility and balance in your life as you navigate tough situations. In this chapter, we explore the importance of resilience, how to build it, and how to use adversity as a stepping stone to greater strength and self-understanding.

Understanding the Components of Resilience

Resilience is not a trait that people either have or do not have. It involves behaviors, thoughts, and actions that can be learned and developed by anyone. Key components of resilience include:

1. Emotional Awareness:

Understanding and managing your emotions helps you respond effectively to stress and recover from setbacks more quickly.

2. Perseverance:

Persistence in the face of challenges and the ability to push through barriers without giving up.

3. Optimism:

Viewing life with a positive outlook and expecting good things to happen, even in difficult times.

4. Flexibility:

The ability to adapt to changing circumstances and think about solutions in innovative ways.

5. Social Support:

Building strong, positive relationships that provide encouragement and affirmation.

Strategies for Building Resilience

Building resilience is a personal journey that involves developing positive attitudes and behaviors. Here are some strategies to help you enhance your resilience:

1. Maintain a Positive Outlook:

Focus on the good aspects of any situation and look for lessons or opportunities for growth. Optimism is a choice that can lead to better outcomes.

2. Establish Goals and Move Towards Them:

Set realistic goals and take small, manageable steps toward achieving them. This helps maintain direction and increases your sense of purpose.

3. Take Decisive Actions:

Act on adverse situations as much as you can. Taking decisive actions rather than detaching completely from problems and stresses helps build a sense of competence.

4. Look for Opportunities for Self-Discovery:

People often learn something about themselves in difficult situations and may find that they have grown in some respect as a result of their struggle.

5. Nurture a Positive Self-View:

Develop confidence in your ability to solve problems and trust your instincts helps build resilience.

6. Keep Things in Perspective:

Even when facing painful events, try to consider the stressful situation in a broader context and keep a long-term perspective.

7. Maintain a Hopeful Outlook:

An optimistic outlook enables you to expect that good things will happen in your life. Try visualizing what you want, rather than worrying about what you fear.

8. Take Care of Yourself:

Pay attention to your own needs and feelings. Engage in activities that you enjoy and find relaxing. Exercise regularly, keeping yourself mentally and physically primed to deal with situations that require resilience.

9. Seek Help When Needed:

Asking for help and seeking guidance is a sign of strength. Talk about your situation with trusted friends, family, or professionals who can provide support and advice.

Personal Story: Learning Resilience in Prison

Reflecting on my own journey, the time spent in prison was a crucible that forged my resilience. I learned to maintain hope and positivity in a place that often felt designed to strip away all dignity. Through emotional awareness and persistence, I developed the ability to look beyond my immediate circumstances and focus on rebuilding my life upon release.

The Role of Resilience in Overcoming Adversity

Building resilience helps not only to manage and overcome existing problems but also to prepare for future challenges. Resilient individuals are better able to maintain their composure and optimism, even in the face of a crisis.

Conclusion: Embracing Resilience for a Fulfilling Life

I was today years old when I realized the full power of resilience. As we close this chapter, remember that resilience is not a passive quality, but an active pursuit. Challenges will come, but with resilience, you have the capacity to meet them head-on, grow from them, and emerge stronger. Use the strategies discussed in this chapter to cultivate your resilience and transform adversity into a powerful source of personal triumph.

Chapter 11: Cultivating Leadership: From Personal Success to Influencing Others

Introduction to Leadership

Leadership is not just about holding a position of power but about inspiring and motivating others toward a common goal. It involves vision, initiative, patience, respect, and the ability to influence others. In this chapter, we'll explore how personal growth can transition into effective leadership and how to use your journey of transformation to inspire and lead others.

The Essence of Leadership

True leadership stems from the ability to translate personal experiences and lessons into strategies that guide and inspire others. It's about setting an example through your behavior and decisions, which in turn influences those around you. Leadership is built on a foundation of trust, integrity, and communication and thrives on the willingness to be vulnerable and authentic.

Key Leadership Qualities

To evolve from personal success to a leadership role, certain qualities are essential:

1. Empathy:

Understanding and sharing the feelings of others, which helps in forging strong connections and addressing team members' concerns effectively.

2. Vision:

Having a clear idea of what you want to achieve and the ability to communicate it clearly and persuasively to others.

3. Communication:

Being able to clearly and effectively express ideas, and also listen actively to others, fostering an environment of open dialogue.

4. Adaptability:

The ability to adjust your approach or strategy based on changing circumstances, without losing sight of the end goal.

5. Integrity:

Sticking to your values and principles, no matter the situation, which earns you respect and loyalty from your team.

Building Leadership Skills

Developing effective leadership skills requires conscious effort and dedication. Here are some strategies to enhance your leadership capabilities:

1. Continuous Learning:

Commit to lifelong learning by reading, attending workshops, and seeking mentorship. This not only broadens your knowledge but also keeps you adaptable and prepared for new challenges.

2. Lead by Example:

Demonstrate the qualities you want to see in your team members. By embodying reliability, hard work, and integrity, you inspire your team to uphold these standards.

3. Empower Others:

Provide opportunities for your team to grow and excel. This means delegating responsibility and avoiding micromanagement, which builds confidence and competence in the team.

4. Foster a Positive Environment:

Create a culture of positivity and encouragement. Recognize achievements, provide constructive feedback, and support your team in their professional and personal growth.

5. Address Conflicts Wisely:

Handle conflicts with fairness and neutrality, seeking to understand all sides and make decisions that are best for the team and the project.

6. Practice Self-Reflection:

Regularly assess your leadership style, decisions, and actions. This self-reflection will help you understand your strengths and areas for improvement.

Personal Story: Transitioning to Leadership

Reflecting on my own transition from following to leading, I recognize that my experiences, particularly those challenging times in prison, equipped me with unique insights into human behavior, perseverance, and the importance of hope and vision. I used these lessons to motivate my team and drive us toward shared successes.

Conclusion: Leading with Purpose

As you develop your leadership skills, remember that the goal is not just to lead but to lead with purpose. Influence others not just to achieve goals, but to foster their own growth and aspirations. Leadership is a journey of continual learning and adaptation, not a destination.

I was today years old when I fully grasped the depth of responsibility and opportunity that comes with leadership. Use your journey, your transformation, and your resilience to inspire those around you to achieve more than what they believe is possible. This is the essence of true leadership.

Chapter 12: Expanding Your Impact: Networking and Community Engagement

Introduction to Networking and Community Involvement

In this chapter, we explore how expanding your personal and professional network, and engaging with your community, can amplify your impact and accelerate your success. Networking and community involvement are pivotal in creating opportunities, fostering relationships, and building a strong support system that can propel you and others toward shared goals.

The Importance of Networking

Networking is more than just exchanging business cards or connecting on social media; it's about building mutually beneficial relationships over time. These relationships can provide support, advice, new perspectives, and access to resources that might not otherwise be available.

Key Networking Strategies

To effectively expand your network, consider the following strategies:

1. Be Genuine:

Approach networking with sincerity. Aim to build relationships based on trust and mutual respect, rather than just the benefits you can gain.

2. Provide Value:

Always think about how you can help others in your network. This could be as simple as offering your expertise, making an introduction, or supporting a colleague's project.

3. Stay Consistent:

Regular interaction is key. Keep in touch through emails, social media, or face-to-face meetings to maintain and strengthen relationships.

4. Attend Events:

Participate in industry conferences, seminars, and local community meetings. These are excellent opportunities to meet new people and learn about ongoing projects and needs within your field.

5. Follow Up:

After meeting someone new, follow up with a note or an email expressing your appreciation for their time and discussing any potential areas for collaboration.

Community Engagement

Engaging with your community not only helps build your network but also enriches your life and the lives of others. It provides a platform for sharing your skills and knowledge, contributing to society's wellbeing, and promoting positive change.

Effective Community Engagement Techniques

1. Volunteer:

Offer your time and skills to local non-profits, schools, or other organizations that align with your values and interests.

2. Participate in Local Governance:

Attend town hall meetings or join local boards to contribute to decision-making processes that affect your community.

3. Organize Events:

Host workshops, talks, or networking events that bring people together and foster a sense of community and collaboration.

4. Support Local Businesses:

Use your influence to promote and support local enterprises, which helps strengthen the local economy.

5. Advocate:

Use your voice and platform to advocate for community issues that need attention, rallying support and resources to cause positive change.

Personal Story: Networking and Community Building

Drawing from my own experiences, I learned the power of networking during my transition back into society. Building connections within various groups helped me not only reintegrate but also find avenues to give back and support others facing similar challenges. These relationships proved invaluable in both my personal growth and professional success.

Conclusion: Beyond Individual Success

As you build your network and engage with your community, remember that your actions do not just benefit you; they also have the potential to impact others positively. Networking and community involvement are about creating a legacy of influence and support that transcends individual accomplishments.

I was today years old when I realized the true power of a supportive network and an engaged community. These elements can transform personal victories into broader societal gains, creating environments where others can thrive alongside you. Embrace these opportunities, and watch as your personal and professional worlds expand in ways you never imagined.

Chapter 13: Overcoming Setbacks: Strategies for Staying the Course

Introduction to Handling Setbacks

Setbacks are an inevitable part of any journey toward success. They test our resolve, challenge our adaptability, and ultimately contribute to our growth. This chapter delves into understanding setbacks, learning from them, and developing strategies to overcome them, ensuring they become stepping stones rather than stumbling blocks on your path to success.

The Nature of Setbacks

Setbacks can vary widely in form and intensity, from minor disappointments like missing a target at work, to major life disruptions such as financial loss or personal crises. Regardless of their scale, the impact of these challenges can significantly affect your momentum and confidence.

Key Strategies to Overcome Setbacks

To effectively deal with setbacks and continue moving forward, consider implementing the following strategies:

1. Acceptance:

Acknowledge that setbacks are a normal part of life. Accepting the situation helps you to move past denial and towards solutions.

2. Reframe Your Perspective:

View setbacks as opportunities for growth and learning rather than as failures. This shift in mindset can transform challenges into valuable experiences.

3. Break Problems Down:

Analyze the setback to understand its components. Breaking it down into manageable parts can make it easier to address each aspect systematically.

4. Develop a Plan:

Once you understand the setback, create a plan to overcome it. Setting short-term goals within this plan can provide quick wins and help rebuild confidence.

5. Seek Support:

Don't face setbacks alone. Reach out to mentors, peers, or a support network for advice and encouragement.

6. Maintain Flexibility:

Be prepared to adjust your strategies as new information and resources become available. Adaptability is key to overcoming unexpected challenges.

7. Practice Resilience:

Strengthen your resilience by maintaining a positive outlook, focusing on your strengths, and not dwelling on the difficulties longer than necessary.

8. Reflect and Learn:

After addressing the setback, take time to reflect on what happened and why. Use these insights to improve future strategies and prevent similar issues.

Real-Life Application: Adapting to Change

Reflecting on my own life, I recall facing a significant setback when transitioning from prison back to civilian life. The skills and mindset that were necessary inside did not translate seamlessly to the outside world. By applying the strategies above—particularly acceptance and developing a plan—I managed to recalibrate my approach to meet the demands of this new phase of life.

Conclusion: Embracing Setbacks as Growth Opportunities

As we wrap up this chapter, remember that setbacks are not just obstacles but are integral to the process of achieving success. They are, in fact, indicators that you are pushing beyond your comfort zone and striving towards meaningful goals.

I was today years old when I truly understood that embracing setbacks as part of your journey can transform them from sources of frustration into sources of enlightenment and empowerment. Keep these strategies in mind as you continue to navigate your path, and let each challenge teach you a little more about yourself and the resilience you possess.

Conclusion: Embracing the Journey with Resilience and Support

As we bring this book to a close, let us take a moment to reflect on the profound journey you've embarked upon by turning these pages. From recognizing the need for change in your mindset and habits, to embracing leadership roles and engaging with your community, each chapter has been crafted to guide you through transforming not just your own life, but also the lives of those around you.

Overcoming the Fear of Failure

Every setback you encounter, every obstacle that blocks your path, is an opportunity—however hidden it might be—to learn, grow, and better prepare for the next challenge. Remember, when something goes wrong, as it inevitably will, it could indeed be worse because it has been worse. In moments of despair, consider the perspective of someone on their deathbed, yearning for just one more chance to make things right, to live fully, to try just once more. You have that chance right now.

The Value of Perspective

This perspective is invaluable. It transforms fear of failure into a motivational force. Fear then becomes not a cage trapping you in inactivity, but a reminder of the finite nature of life and the infinite possibilities that courage can unlock. Embrace the fear of failing as a lesser evil compared to the regret of never having tried.

You Are Not Alone

Perhaps most importantly, remember: you are not alone on this journey. I am here with you, not just as an author of a book, but as someone who has navigated the treacherous waters of change and transformation against formidable odds. I've faced darkness, setbacks, and despair, but I've also witnessed the sunrise of success and fulfillment that follows perseverance.

Promise of Support

As you set out to achieve your goals—knowing well that the path will not be easy—take heart in knowing that my experiences, insights, and encouragement are with you. I have your back. This book is more than a collection of chapters; it is a companion on your journey. Use it as a beacon when the way forward seems dim, as a shield when challenges arise, and as a reminder of the community and network that supports you.

Call to Action

So, as you close this book, do not see it as the end of your reading, but as the commencement of your doing. Step out with the knowledge that the journey to achievement is paved with trials, but each trial is surmountable. Your dreams are valid, your goals achievable, and the impact you can have on the world is profound.

Stand up now. Move forward with determination. The fear of failure is indeed better than the reflection on what could have been. You have all the tools you need, and with resilience and a supportive community, there is no limit to what you can accomplish. Together, let's move forward, embracing every challenge, celebrating every victory, and always, always pushing towards the greater good.

I was today years old when I saw clearly that every new day is a fresh opportunity to make a difference. Let's make it count.

www.ingramcontent.com/pod-product-compliance
Lightning Source LLC
Chambersburg PA
CBHW082221220526
45470CB00010B/3254